Reviews

"*Be Her Now* encourages women to be happier by being a nuisance to society."
– *Denali Marsch (male high school student)*

"Because white ladies have problems, too."
– *Some white lady*

"If only I had read *Be Her Now* BEFORE I followed my husband down
that stupid golden escalator in 2015."
– *Mrs. Trump (for now)*

"For the love of God, someone stop my daughter."
– *Lynn's mother*

"I'm so busy with my wonderfully fulfilling career, my perfect family
and my daily yoga practice, I don't have time – or need – for this book,
but I think it will be good for you."
– *That one "friend" you need to drop already*

"I did not read *Be Her Now* so I cannot endorse it. Also, I did not write this review."
– *Ruth Bader Ginsberg*

"Just buy the damn thing and you'll see – it helps! Plus,
it's short and there are cartoons so your lips won't get tired reading it.
Please make the check out to 'cash.'"
– *Someone who looks a lot like Lynn but isn't her*

Be Her Now

The Most Important Job
of Every Woman

Flying Heart Industries

Anchorage, Alaska

The author is grateful for permission to reprint the following copyrighted material:
Excerpt from *Revolution from Within: A Book of Self-Esteem* by Gloria Steinem.
Copyright © 1992, 1993 by Gloria Steinem. Used by permission of Little Brown and Company.
Excerpt from *The Feminine Mystique* by Betty Friedan. Copyright © 1983, 1974, 1973, 1963 by Betty Friedan. Used by permission of W.W. Norton & Company, Inc.
Excerpt from *Man's Search for Meaning* by Viktor E. Frankl. Copyright ©1959, 1962, 1984, 1992 by Viktor E. Frankl. Used by permission of Beacon Press, Boston.

Cataloguing-in-Publication Data available from the Library of Congress.
ISBN: 978-1-7323800-1-1 (paperback)
ISBN: 978-1-7323800-0-4 (e-book)
ISBN: 978-1-7323800-2-8 (Kindle)

Book design by Anelise Schutz
Illustrations by Lynn E. Paulson
Author photo by Dan Barsotti and Lynn E. Paulson. All other photos from Paulson Family Collection.
Be Her Now ™ is a registered trademark of Lynn E. Paulson and Flying Heart Industries, all rights reserved.

flying Heart Industries

10 9 8 7 6 5 4 3 2 1

For my parents,
Peggy and Stan, Marcia and Robert,
who made me what I am today.
With love.

The woman who does not require validation from anyone is the most feared individual on the planet.[1]

– Mohadesa Najumi

Be Her Now.

– Lynn Edith Paulson

Contents

Preface

The first draft of *Be Her Now* was both hand-drawn and written. The choice to use large, printed letters, crude drawings and to have only a few words on any page wasn't entirely conscious, I don't think. But as I later realized, months after the second draft of the book was already done, it wasn't exactly an accident, either.

It was an early spring day in Anchorage, Alaska, and I was navigating my car through the cracking street ice, bouncing in and out of deep potholes filled with slush, when I suddenly remembered where I had first seen a book with a style like the original draft of this one.

When I was six, my father brought a book home for me in his suitcase when he returned from a business trip. The book, published in 1965, was written by Morris Sand and illustrated by Leonard Glasser. It was called *That's Ugly*.

That's Ugly had a brown cover and the title was rendered in a large, black scrawl. The drawings within were rough and the few words accompanying each one were printed in giant font. So if you only skimmed the first few pages, if you were in a hurry, say, because you had a plane to catch, you might not realize that *That's Ugly* was not a book for children.

It would be years before I knew, for example, what the words "venereal disease" meant ("Ugly is an ice cream man with venereal disease. That's Ugly." p. 51), and yet I somehow knew, even then, that what I held in my six-year-old hands was a masterpiece of comic outrage.

In the decades that have since passed I have probed the darker recesses of my memory more than once and can say with certainty for all time that my father never got past page three of *That's Ugly* or I would never have come into possession of what this man, my father, had in his haste judged an appropriate gift for his young daughter. The fact that this happened could have come straight from its pages:

> *Ugly is a father who gives his child a book with a drawing of a*
> *Good Humor Ice Cream man with a chancre on his mouth handing*
> *out Popsicles and Eskimo Pies to little children. That's Ugly.*

Like I said, at six, I didn't understand everything I read in the pages of *That's Ugly*, but as I read it from cover to cover that night in my room, I caught on to something my father didn't when he purchased the present that I had demanded he bring me:

That's Ugly was irreverent.

It was naughty.

It didn't follow the rules.

At six, based on the sheer volume of notes I brought home to my parents from my teachers and the hours I spent in the principal's office, I already knew that those things were true about me as well.

I recognized a kindred soul in Morris Sand, and it was from his book I first began to understand that there were ways to express myself and the truth as I saw it that were outrageous, profane, playful and deeply honest all at the same time. In my earlier career as a college professor, in my work as a writer, and, more recently, as a life coach, I have continued to witness how difficult truths or contentious and thorny issues, when approached in ways that are both provocative and funny, are easier to address, to hear, and to deal with.

When we laugh, our hearts are open.

When our hearts are open, we can heal what is broken.

INTRODUCTION

*The idea for this book began a dozen years ago
when even I, who had spent the previous dozen
years working on external barriers to women's
equality, had to admit there were internal
ones, too...*[1]

– Gloria Steinem

INTRODUCTION

A few years ago, I did a mad thing ...

I base-jumped out of a comfortable, middle-class, home-owning life, leaving over 20 years of a successful, professional career behind me. I left steady work at a decent wage that did more than sustain me. I left a job that came with good benefits. I left a job that came with more freedom and ownership of my time than most people will ever have in their entire professional lives. More than that?

I left a job that I *liked.*
With *colleagues* I liked.
With colleagues I *respected.*
When the economy was in the toilet.

WTF, right???

But wait —
There's more!!!

Not only did I quit my job, I left a marriage that wasn't working. I gave away, donated or sold almost everything I owned, including my house.

I left town.

It was nothing less than my mother's worst nightmare and in my imagination I could hear her howling at me from beyond the grave ...

The madness had actually started a few years earlier, on my birthday. That night, I scribbled the following sentence at the top of a clean page in my journal:

Not this one →

Jan 15

Today I ate nothing but cheese and bacon. Cheese and bacon. Cheese and bacon cheese and bacon. Today I ate cheese and bacon till I thought I would explode. Not my finest hour...

Jan 16

From now on, I will live and speak my truth...

← This one

I was so surprised that I stopped writing and sat back to contemplate the ten words that had seemingly bubbled up from my unconscious, unbidden, and worked their way onto the page from the pen in my hand:

From now on I will live and speak my truth?

What *was* my truth? And what exactly had I *been* doing?

To be honest, that wasn't an especially difficult question to answer. Like many women I knew, what I genuinely thought, how I truly felt and what I really wanted were not always reflected directly, or even reliably, in what I said or did.

I wanted people to like me.
I didn't want to make them angry.
I didn't want them to judge or reject me.

This compelled me to hide or distort my truth and misrepresent myself in various ways in order to maintain their approval and good will.

Like you've
- never done
that...

Oh, sure, I spoke loudly and with confidence, yes. To all appearances, I seemed forthright, independent and self-assured. Brash, even. That's certainly how most people would have described me.

Truthfully, I was a pleaser. And if I took an honest look at my
life, the evidence was all around me:

Two injudicious marriages.

The job I loved was becoming an unchallenging routine.

I spent way too much time doing things
I didn't want with people I didn't like.

Did I mention
I was eating pain-killers
like Pez?

I knew my life had been built upon the choices I'd made over the years, but that night I recognized that some of those choices were based to a degree I could not ignore on my need for approval and positive regard from other people. As successful as my life appeared to be by any ordinary standards, and as much as it had satisfied me for many years, it had begun to feel like a cage in which I could no longer stand up.

My TRUTH?

Immediately, I could hear the shrill voice of that bitch, Convention, making her way down the hallway in my head in her sensible shoes, shaking a finger at me and mocking me with that scornful question:

Even though it was a rhetorical question, intended to shame and scare me into staying right where I was and sticking things out, I realized I had a choice:

Leaving behind the security of the life I had, especially as the economy was tanking, was risky. I knew that people would judge me insane, stupid or both. But I decided that night that whatever was left of my life belonged to me.

Fuck 'em.

Instead of being controlled by my fears, I decided to listen to my heart. I would follow the directive of my journal – living and speaking my truth – and pay close attention to what happened when I didn't. I would find the courage to go ahead and answer that question –

JUST WHO THE HELL DO I THINK I AM?

– in earnest.

It was the best birthday present I ever gave myself.

It also scared the shit out of me.

(But I went ahead and did it anyway.)

I wrote *Be Her Now* because way too often, due to fear, insecurity, our need to please and all the other pressures of our social programming, **She**, the almighty woman we are inside, and the woman we present to the world are not the same person.

Be Her Now is about loving **Her** fiercely and being **Her** without apology. *Be Her Now* is about bringing all **Her** game to the table because this is key to the most meaningful and satisfying life possible, to being more effective in, and of greater service to, the world.

Creating this book was a much more challenging task than I ever imagined, not least of all because I wrote *Be Her Now* while I was in the midst of learning how to do it.

And FYI? The learning never stops.

(More about that later.)

I'm making no claim here to speak for all women in this book. *Be Her Now* is written with my most affluent sisters in mind, we privileged women here in America and the other gated communities of the industrialized world who have access to books, the money to buy them and the time to read them.

I wrote *Be Her Now* for those of us who enjoy freedom and distance from warfare, persecution, poverty and the immediate threats to survival like a lack of food, clean water, shelter and medical care.

I wrote *Be Her Now* for those of us who aren't living where violence toward females is openly sanctioned and practiced or where females are denied a basic education as a matter of cultural practice and tradition.

I wrote *Be Her Now* for my friends, my clients, my students, for all of us who, by reason of our immense good fortune, opportunities and resources, bear the greatest responsibility for advancing the cause of freedom for women everywhere.

Where do we begin?

By slipping the collar and leash we've put around our own necks.

My goal is to convince you
that this is a good idea.

That it's not only necessary.

It's urgent.

I'm not assuming here that the experience of being female is the same for all of us. Class, race, nationality, sexuality and a multitude of other differences shape our lives in distinct and significant ways. *Be Her Now* focuses on the social conditioning we share as females and the way it hides inside our heads, telling us to shut up and behave ourselves and pretend to be someone we're not.

Our Feminist Foremothers unlocked the door to the social and political freedoms you and I enjoy today. But even now, even here, we can't take those freedoms for granted. Each woman still has to choose for herself to walk through that door, living and speaking her truth.

As simple as that sounds, you and I both know it can be one of the most frightening, radical, outrageous and provocative things any of us can do. It is nothing less than a political act with profound personal implications. It requires courage and a commitment to overcome a lifetime of brainwashing.

IT CAN
ALSO BE FUN!

Part I:
OUR STORY

The eyes of others, our prisons; their thoughts, our cages.[1]

– Virginia Woolf

Our Story

This is a small book about a big, big problem. Betty Friedan called it "The Problem That Has No Name." She published a book about The Problem in 1963.

The problem that has no name – which is simply the fact that American women are kept from growing to their full human capacities – is taking a far greater toll on the physical and mental health of our country than any known disease.[2]

– Betty Friedan, *The Feminine Mystique*

Betty was writing about herself and her peers, a generation of college-educated (and mostly white) women who had achieved The American Dream.

You know the one.

They had it all.

The house. The car. The Don Draper.
The 2.5 kids and the time-saving appliances.

Only a lot of them didn't seem all that happy about it.

They seemed to be drinking a lot more.

And they were using more mood-altering prescription drugs.

And their kids were having more "accidents."

They were showing up in significant numbers in doctors'
and psychiatrists' offices with vague complaints and nothing
really "wrong" with them.

It was easy for individual women who "had it all" but were frustrated and unsatisfied to believe that *they* were the source of The Problem. Their husbands, families, doctors and other "experts" thought so, too.

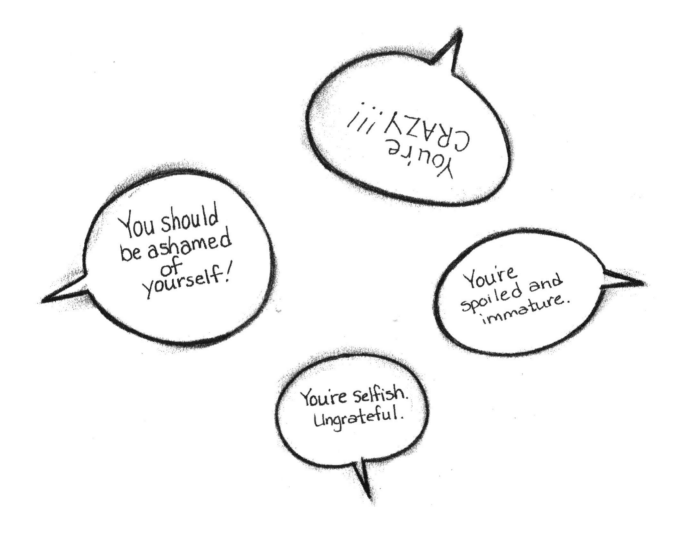

Women *did* feel guilty. They *did* feel shame. They *felt* selfish and ungrateful. Spoiled. Immature. Crazy. Women felt all those things and they also felt alone because they weren't talking to each other about The Problem.

Betty Friedan had a different point of view on The Problem. Like the other, early founders of Second Wave Feminism, she believed that the quality of women's lives depends directly on the beliefs, values, practices and policies of the culture in which they live, especially as they pertain to women.

And when it came to those beliefs, values, practices and policies?

The mystique of passive, inferior femininity?
Wasting women's educations, talents and lives?

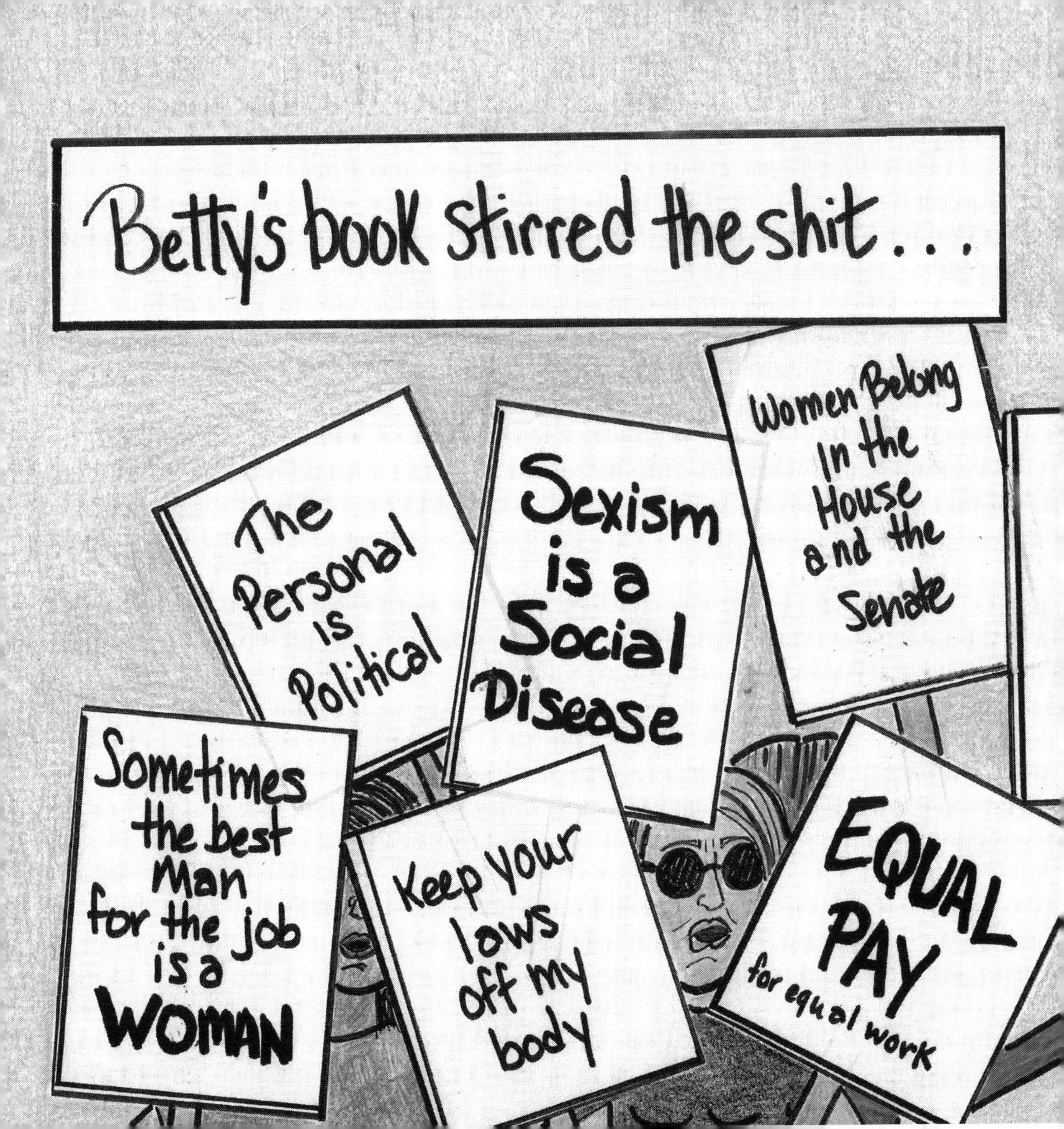
Betty's book stirred the shit . . .
The Personal is Political
Sexism is a Social Disease
Women Belong In the House and the Senate
Sometimes the best Man for the job is a WOMAN
Keep your laws off my body
EQUAL PAY for equal work

Women behaved badly and made history.

They changed the law.

They changed the culture.

But women's work?

Never done.

Yes, there has been progress.

But the world of women is more than just us. Appalling crimes are being committed against women and girls all over the world every single day.

The closest you and I get to it is watching documentaries on Netflix and YouTube.

Women like us?

Our lives are a whole different kind of fucked up.

Let's assess, shall we?

Today, we have greater access to opportunities, resources and influence in every area of life!

But we are suffering unprecedented rates of depression, alcoholism, drug addiction, obesity and a host of other physical and mental health problems.

Today, we have a voice in every cultural institution!

But it can feel like a minor act of bravery to say what we really think, what we truly want or how we actually feel in our personal lives.

Today, we are contributing to groundbreaking discoveries that improve life on our planet and expand the boundaries of human knowledge!

But we aren't comfortable speaking up when our own boundaries are violated.

We don't respect or value our truth like we should.

We don't take care of ourselves half as well as we take care of other people.

Our relationship with ourselves is too often the most dysfunctional relationship we have.

The bottom line?

The Problem That Has No Name is the Problem that Hasn't Gone Away

The Problem for the past several decades has been this –

Feminism has been seen as:

Ugly.
Angry.
Irrational.
Irrelevant.
Unstylish.

Beginning in the late 90's or early 2000's, I began to hear my female students say things like:

OMG. Feminism is <u>so</u> OVER.!!

That battle has been <u>won</u>.

But women have equal rights now.

I've never experienced sexism in my life...

Yes. Yes, you do, I would say. You do experience sexism in your life.

And then I would explain how when sexism, racism and other forms of discrimination are against the law, they don't just disappear. They slither underground, where they're less obvious and harder to explain, especially to the people who don't experience them and don't want to believe they exist.

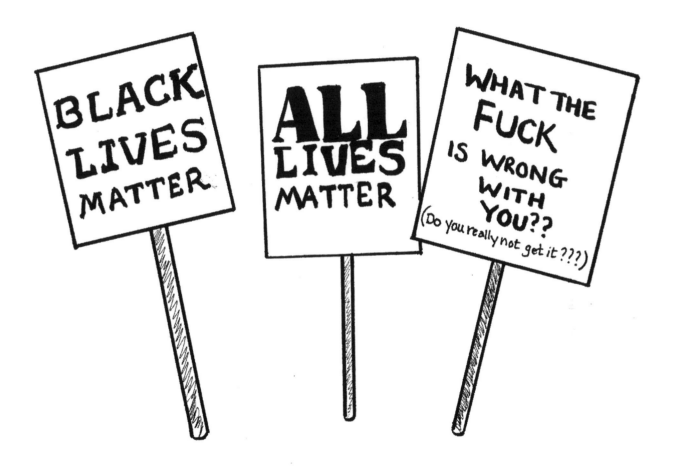

Women like you and I aren't openly "policed" like we once were in order to keep us in line and "in our place."

But we don't have to be.

We do the job ourselves.

A new movement is afoot right now, yes. FINALLY.
It's a start. And it gives me hope.

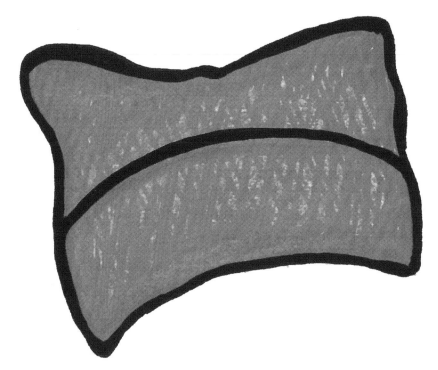

And yet?

We still pretend that these are not the eyes through which we look at ourselves.

We still judge ourselves against cultural standards that instruct us to be younger, smaller, more attractive, nicer and quieter than we are. We throw away too much money on products that are garbage and procedures that are painful and risky and rarely convincing. We waste a lot of time and energy worrying about whether or not we measure up.

We still don't respond to the world around us spontaneously and authentically, like empowered human beings. Instead, we run things past a committee of voices in our heads that debate what's expected, what's at stake and what will keep us in the good graces of other people.

And *then* we respond.

(It's such an automatic process that it happens, roughly, in a nanosecond.)

We betray ourselves all day long by trying to please others, to avoid their criticism, anger and rejection by meeting standards we didn't define and by following "the rules" we didn't create. This has become the Prime Directive. We do this because we think it makes us safe.

In reality, it allows others to define us, and our worth, for their own purposes. It alienates us from our own truth and our real value.

It kills our very souls.

Does that sound "safe" to you?

Be Her Now is about how women think about ourselves and present ourselves to the world.

Be Her Now is about how the world thinks about women and presents us to ourselves.

Be Her Now is about how we are in deep shit on both counts.

Be Her Now is about how She, the glorious and fabulous and POWERFUL bitch we are inside, and the woman we present to the world are not the same woman often enough.

Be Her Now is about loving Her fiercely and letting Her outside for the world to see Her, hear Her and deal with Her, because She needs to be seen and She's worth listening to.

Be Her Now is about the relationship between a woman's truth and her self-esteem.

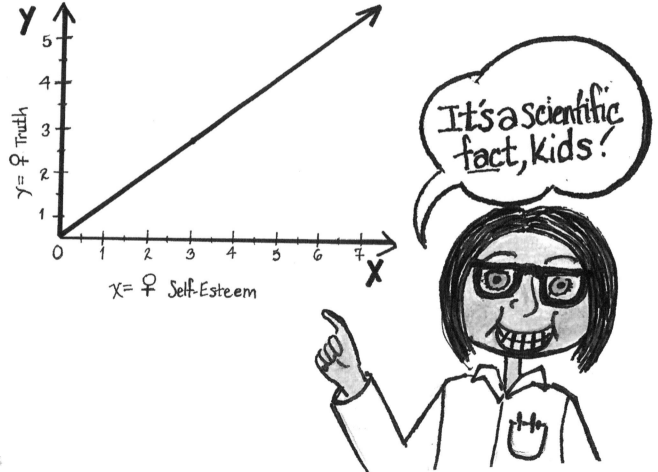

Be Her Now is about how loving and celebrating and being Her improves the very quality of our lives and the lives of the people around us.

How so?

Because She holds the key to the truth of who you are, the work you are meant to do and the life you are meant to lead.

Because She holds the key to your greater fulfillment.

Because She holds the key to being of greatest service to others.

But the world doesn't want to know Her, does it? It doesn't want to hear Her truth.

So if you're a woman in search of a program to be Her, to help you learn to live and speak your deep truth as a way to strengthening your sense of self-worth and living the largest, most meaningful life possible...

Sorry.

Be Her Now is not that kind of book.

Be Her Now contains no:

1. Programs.
2. Checklists.
3. Affirmations.
4. Exercises.
5. Nuts of any kind.

The last thing you or I or any woman needs is one more program to fix what's "wrong" with us or with our lives.

Programming *is* The Problem.

Be Her Now is not a guidebook for fixing a specific problem you think you have.

It's not about self-improvement.

Fuck self-improvement.

Be Her Now is about how
you roll in life.

Be Her Now is for women who want to follow their **own** path, to set their **own** standards, and to trust, and draw inspiration and strength from, **their own inner guidance.**

Being Her Now is a lifelong journey with no maps. There is no finish line that you need to cross in a set amount of time. Charting your own course is the point, the very thing that gives you the strength, confidence and courage to Be Her Now.

You should expect to get lost in the swamp.

You should expect to find your way out again.

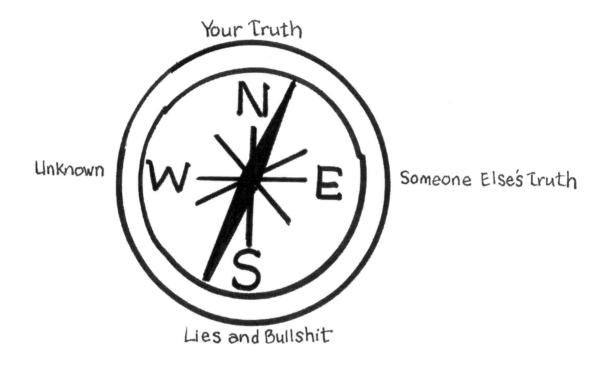

You will learn as you go that your own inner guidance is the finest compass you could ever have and you will begin to trust it more and more and move in the direction it points because of the results it gives you.

So why the hell are you reading *Be Her Now*?

1. Simple navigation tools.
2. Fresh eyes for crossing the terrain.
3. Where to expect, and how to prepare for, enemy ambush.

Are you ready?

Let's rock and roll.

Part II:
WHO IS SHE?

The real power behind whatever success I have now was something I found within myself – something that's in all of us – a little piece of God waiting to be discovered.[1]

– Tina Turner

Who is She?

Let's start with my story...

Although my family sometimes thought
I came from The Devil...

In reality, I came from Berkeley.

January, 1959.

Cocktail hour.

My scared young mother and father
were graduate students there.

And they weren't married.

1. I was conceived on Easter weekend, in a cold mountain stream (His).

We were engaged to be married.

2. I was conceived in a dorm room after they attended a reading by T.S. Elliot (Hers).

We were engaged to be married.

In any case, they did
The Sensible Thing.

Sensible Thing

I was so young when my mom and dad told me I was adopted that I don't remember ever **not** knowing. Being adopted never felt shameful to me. My parents said that being adopted meant I was chosen. I was wanted.

I was in the company of **Moses.**

So for me, being adopted was always like membership in a very exclusive club. I felt sorry for kids who arrived in their families in the usual way.

In the fairytale version of events...

Well, mostly safe.

In reality, it was three months before my adopted parents could bring me home from the hospital. I was sick. And I kept getting sicker. Basically, I was just doing what newborns deprived of touch and bonding will do – failing to thrive. If they survive, they tend to be anxious, fearful, and hard to comfort.

When my new parents were finally able to bring me home, I screamed and screamed and SCREAMED, driving my new, big brother insane and my nervous mother right behind him. I screamed until I PASSED OUT. You could say we got off to a rough start.

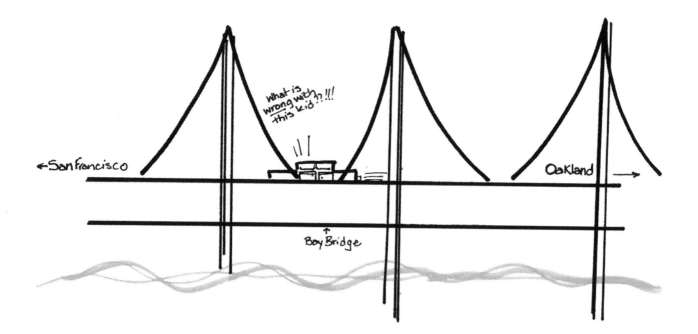

Eventually, I settled down, but in the meantime, my brother's worst suspicions were confirmed. No good could possibly come from this new arrangement.

We went to war immediately.

Oh, I know. You're probably wondering what chance did I possibly have against an opponent four years older and at least three times my size, right?

HA!

I learned to walk so I could get to the knives.

I learned to talk so I could tell on him.

I learned to get him when he was sleeping.

Our poor parents. Such fine people! Such good intentions!
Their marriage was solid. Their future was secure. When
they adopted my brother, they became a family. All they
needed to make this picture "perfect" was a daughter.
Everything had been going according to plan.

I don't think the problem for them was that with my arrival, their house became a war zone. Lots of families are full of kids doing their best to murder each other. I think the problem was that I was not only different from my parents, I was different from my brother, in the same sort of ways.

In the simplest terms possible . . .

Mom, Dad, Brother	Me
Pays Attention	Seeks Attention
Quiet	Never Shuts Up
Low-Key	High Strung
Emotionally Reserved	Anything But …
Steady	Random
Self-Controlled	Impulsive
Demure	Dramatic

Instead of a daughter, my parents had basically adopted a Howler Monkey.

I didn't sleep. I wouldn't stay in bed. Even when, in desperation, my parents locked me in my bedroom so that they could get some sleep, I would talk to them from under the door.

6am, Saturday.
Dear Diary—
 Everything was going smoothly until the chair fell over. Now the baby aspirin is somewhere else.. But where?

After one of my physical check-ups, the pediatrician prescribed tranquilizers for my mother.

I got into everything.
I turned every room I was in upside down.
I had no "OFF" switch.

I wasn't exactly a bad kid or a mean kid, but when it came to school I was always in trouble, constantly bringing home notes from the teacher for fighting or for other crazy stuff I did.

My mom used to say that time takes care of a lot of things, and she was right. The patience and steadying influence of my parents went a long way toward helping me to rein in my more dubious tendencies (mostly). As I got older, I stopped bouncing off the walls and ceiling. I started cultivating self-discipline in school, eventually earning a Ph.D. and becoming a college professor.

Dr. Paulson and Dr. Paulson.

It's also true that whatever else about us changes, the role we play in our family while we're growing up is a lifetime assignment...

No matter how long it takes for you to get over your childhood, your family never will. "Black Sheep," "Howler Monkey," "Problem Child" – whatever the label, it stuck and it stung. Even if the qualities that had driven my family crazy (impulsiveness, for example) had mellowed into something more palatable (spontaneity, say), they felt shameful.

I had a big personality and I felt that, in order to be acceptable, I needed to become smaller, quieter, to suppress certain qualities I had. But no matter how hard I tried to cage the Howler Monkey, she always managed to escape.

And then one day...

The "Incident."

Flash forward to my 30th year. I was home visiting my parents on a semester break. They were acting strange, cagey. Over breakfast on the second morning, I learned why.

We have some information about your biological father...

My mom and dad knew a fair amount about my biological parents and, guided by the questions I had asked them growing up, they shared what they knew. But of all the questions I had asked them over the years, "Do you know the names of my biological parents?" wasn't among them.

But if I *had* asked that question, the answer
would have been "Yes."

my parents
were in possession
of my original
birth certificate
all along.

A few months earlier my dad had been in a bookstore. As he walked past a table piled high with copies of a new, runaway bestseller, he glanced at the name of the author and he recognized it. He bought a copy of the book, brought it home and showed it to my mom, asking her if the name of the author looked familiar to her, too.

It did.

My mom said all she had to do was look at the photo of the author on the back flap of the book jacket.

"And I **knew**," she said.

About a week later, they read an article about the author in *The New York Times Magazine.* It confirmed without a shadow of a doubt what they already knew in their guts to be true.

The author was my father.

As I sat there at the breakfast table that morning listening to their story, it didn't sink in right away what my parents were telling me. I remember feeling outside of my body, far, far away. My mother put the book down in front of me along with a copy of *The New York Times Magazine* with the story about the author. I opened the magazine right to the story and a double-paged photo of the author, sitting on a swing in his living room.

How to even describe the tsunami of emotions I felt at that moment, staring at a face like my own for the first time in my life?

Primal recognition.

Shock.

Utter hilarity.

The mental image of the last piece of a jigsaw puzzle, the very center, sliding gently into place, followed by an immediate understanding that my life had suddenly changed forever.

My mom asked me if I thought the author was my biological father.

"I know he is," I said, and I burst into tears.

My parents told me that they would support me in whatever I wanted to do with the information they had just given me. To this day, I can't think of a more generous act on the part of my mom and dad as adoptive parents, especially because they knew me well enough to know I would want to meet my birth parents.

They assured me before I could even ask for their blessing that they were perfectly secure in the knowledge that they, and no one else, could ever be my mom and dad.

I never felt a need to search for my birth parents growing up but I understood from the time I was fairly young that giving up a baby was a devastating thing for anyone to do, even if it was the right decision. I had always wished I could somehow reassure my birth parents that I was okay.

And so, as a kid, I used to lie on my back on the grass and talk to them, Kinda the way other people talk to God.

Now, suddenly, I had the information I needed in order to try and track them down and tell them I was okay. Finding them turned out to be an incredibly easy process and by nightfall, I had my first conversation with both my birth mother and father.

Among the things I learned that night:

1. They were married for 13 years, and then divorced.
2. They had two sons, a daughter and the grandchildren were starting to arrive.
3. Everyone lived in the same city.
4. They had expected me to turn up at some point.
5. They wanted to meet me.

And so, in three days I boarded a plane and walked into a roomful of total strangers who seemed very familiar.

They were boisterous. They were bouncing off the walls and ceiling. They were writers, artists, musicians, teachers, provocateurs and eccentrics who could not fly beneath the radar if their lives depended on it and didn't want to.

People who had no "OFF" switch.

Howler monkeys.

I opened the door to the cage and set my own monkey free.

My point in telling you my story is this –

I have stared the Nature vs. Nurture debate right in the face, and here is what the experience taught me:

You ARE who you ARE.

(SHIT oh dear.)

There's really only one question you have to ask yourself.

What am I going to do about it?

Here's one suggestion.

Be Yourself. Everyone else is already taken.[2]

Author and playwright Oscar Wilde said this, and when it came to being yourself, that's exactly what he did.

In spades. Without apology.

Oscar Wilde was an outrageous and publicly visible personality. He was also a flamboyant homosexual at the turn of the 20th century.

So his suggestion, to be yourself, was more than flip irreverence.

It was the most radical and dangerous idea he could propose, let alone pursue. It was also a cry from the deepest part of his soul and he answered it, even though he knew it would cost him dearly.

But Oscar Wilde also said that it was better to be talked about badly than to not be talked about at all. He knew exactly who he was. Authenticity came at a price he was willing to pay.

Oscar Wilde arrived on the planet as himself and you arrived as you. Circumstances and experiences shape the clay from which you are made. But the clay? The raw material itself?

Never changes.

Option #1:

Make a shitty little ashtray that winds up in the junk drawer in the kitchen.

Option #2:

Do like Oscar Wilde and form it into your personal masterpiece.

To be sure, some people will like it  and some won't. And that's just the way it is.

Different people will judge the same qualities in different ways.

For example:

Exuberant vs. Drama Queen   Direct vs. Asshole
Colorful vs. Weird   Supportive vs. Doormat
Bold vs. Reckless   Happy vs. Shallow
Sociable vs. Blabbermouth   Decisive vs. Impulsive

Which is true?

Both.

Neither.

It doesn't matter. It isn't even the right question.

But it's a question we women tend to worry about a lot.

Am I okay? Do people like me? Am I acceptable? Do they approve?

This keeps us very busy, distracted from more important matters at hand.

And that *does* matter.

Abraham Maslow, a 20th century psychologist, believed that human development progresses through the satisfaction of certain basic, hard-wired needs.

* Maslow's Heirarchy of Needs (1943).

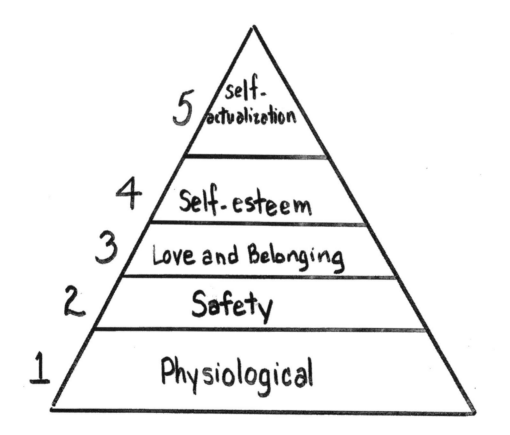

First, we meet our most basic needs, for physical survival (food, water, oxygen) and for safety (from the elements, from physical harm).

Once we've accomplished that, our efforts turn to meeting our need for positive emotional bonds with others, to our need to be accepted by, and belong to, a social group.

From there, human beings seek to meet our need for self-respect or self-esteem, for a sense of worthiness.

Finally, we strive for self-actualization, for achieving our own highest potential.[3]

When it comes to the human need for love and belonging, it's easy for women to get into trouble. We're conditioned from the cradle on up to believe that it's critical for us to please, and win the approval of, others, even if it means behaving in ways that are at odds with, and hide, who we really are.

So where does
She go when
we do this?

She is right there, the whole time, telling us what we *really* want to do, what we *genuinely* think or feel, whispering our deep truth in our ear while we choose instead to do or say things that deny Her and disregard Her wisdom and guidance.

We pay a high price for this.

When we ignore or deny Her, She goes to The Dark Side, poisoning us with insecurity, self-doubt, self-loathing, depression and worse.

When being acceptable to, liked by and pleasing others comes before honoring our own guidance and integrity, we are more likely to make bad choices, to wind up in situations we don't want and don't like, doing things we don't want to do.

Look, do we even need to review here?

I didn't think so...

How do we develop a healthy self-respect and self-esteem when we let this happen, over and over?

How do we develop a healthy sense of our own worth when we repeatedly compromise our own integrity?

How do we realize our own, true potential when we forfeit our lives for the purpose of pleasing others?

Newsflash!

When we get hung up on the approval and judgments of other people, we're putting energy into something over which we have almost no control.

Newsflash!

When we're guided by other people's responses to us, we cannot develop, or hear, our **own** guidance.

Another Newsflash!

We're not meant to have control over the opinions and judgments of other people in the first place.

That's not the point of the exercise.

When it comes to meeting our needs for love and belonging and our needs for self-esteem and a sense of worthiness, please understand that we deserve to have these needs met no matter who we are or what other people think of us.

The point of the exercise is to meet these needs and deal with the judgments of others in healthy, self-respecting ways instead of wasting time and energy trying to "get it right" in their eyes, **which is impossible.**

When we learn to do this, our attention, time and energy can be put toward the more important and meaningful purpose of meeting our 5th basic need, for self-actualization.

Self-actualization comes out of a conscious desire for growth. Here, we seek to maximize our own potential by developing our talents and abilities to the fullest extent possible.

Human development doesn't just end with self-actualization, however.

In a later version of his hierarchy, Maslow included a 6th hard-wired human need, for self-transcendence. Here, attention and energy are directed toward something beyond, and larger than, our individual existence.[4]

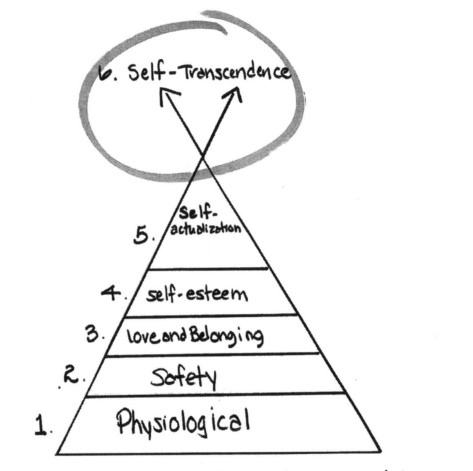

Maslow's Heirarchy of Needs, Revised (1954).

In self-transcendence, we seek to experience our fundamental connection to everyone and everything else, and to understand our place in, and our contribution to, the Bigger Picture.

This something or "Bigger Picture" goes by many names and means different things to different people, including "God."

or

or

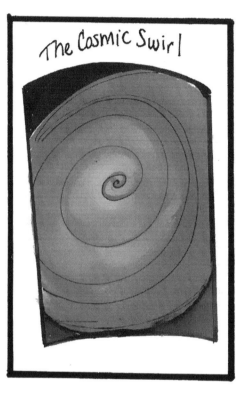

Our Higher Power as We Understand [Him]
Hi Lola!!!...
Hi, I'm Lola and I'm an... alcoholic...
OR
The One.
We are all Juan.
Juan Martinez
Juan Lopez
Juan Diego Arturo

The Divine. The Life Force. Humanity. Buddha Consciousness. Love. The Quantum Energy Field. The Big Wow. Krishna. The Global Village. Spirit. The Bigger Picture, etc.

But not this.

Excuse me?
I'm not the center
— of the Known Universe?
Fuck you.

Your ego.

Viktor Frankl, a 20th century psychiatrist and Holocaust survivor, developed his theory and method for treating depressed and suicidal patients while spending three years as a prisoner in a Nazi concentration camp.

Based on his experiences and observations, he came to believe that people maintain the will to live, even in the most horrific circumstances, when they believe that their life has meaning, when they have a sense of a worthy purpose or mission in life that it is their duty to fulfill. In his 1959 book, *Man's Search For Meaning*, Frankl talks about it this way:

The point is not what we expect from life, but rather what life expects from us... Everyone has his own specific vocation or mission in life to carry out a concrete assignment, which demands fulfillment. Therein he cannot be replaced, nor can his life be repeated... When the impossibility of replacing a person is realized, it allows the responsibility that a man has for his existence and its continuance to appear in all its magnitude.[5]

There will never be another Oscar Wilde.

There will never be another Abraham Maslow.

There will never be another Viktor Frankl.

There will NEVER
be another you.

The odds that there is, that there ever has been, or there ever will be, another person exactly like you are so ridiculously, so infinitesimally small as to be basically zero.

No matter how you think about or define the "something" that is bigger than or beyond you and your life, the picture changes if you're not in it, if the impact you make by being here never happened.

We each have a unique role to play in our time here that is ours and ours alone. Whatever that role is, it is contained in the deepest essence of who we are, in the talents and abilities with which we've been blessed and in the longing of our hearts.

Do you get
that?
You matter.
You are incredibly
precious.

So go ahead and say that to yourself when you are standing on the Evil Bathroom Scale tomorrow morning, because it speaks to a much more important and meaningful truth than the numbers staring up at you.

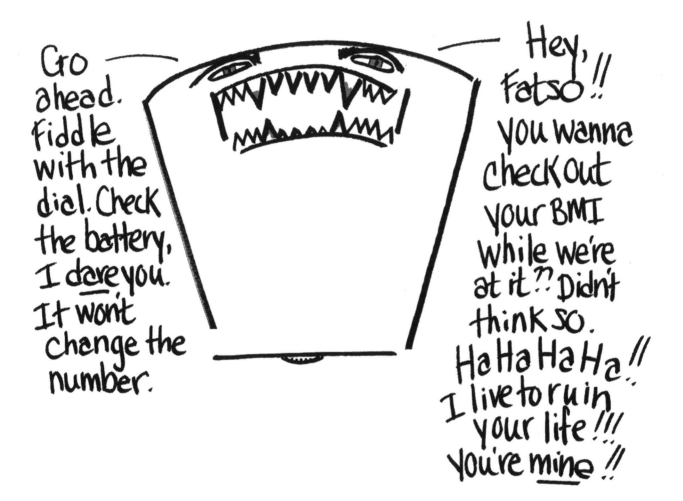

So instead of wishing you were different, treasure the singular truth of who you are. Instead of trying to be someone else, work with what you've got and make it work for you.

Because these are your options.

Because everyone else is already taken.

Because being yourself is what you do best and it's the single thing you are better at doing than anyone else on the planet.

Because being yourself is basically your cosmic job description and your life will be better if this is your operating principle.

The only question is,
what are YOU bringing
to the party?

Part III:
BE HER NOW

You must always be yourself, no matter what the price. It is the highest form of morality.[1]

– Candy Darling

Be Her Now

This is the Prime Directive, the task before women like you and me today – liberating ourselves from the oppressive forces of bullshit that lie within and hold us back in our daily lives so we can get down to more meaningful business.

But what does Be Her Now mean, *specifically*?

That depends on each individual woman and who She is.

When I asked other women what Be Her Now means to them, here are some of the things they said:

L.C. — "When I am Being Her Now, I am at home plate. I am in the best position to see the field, to direct my own life, to choose, to react, and live in the moment with myself and others. Here, I live my true self."

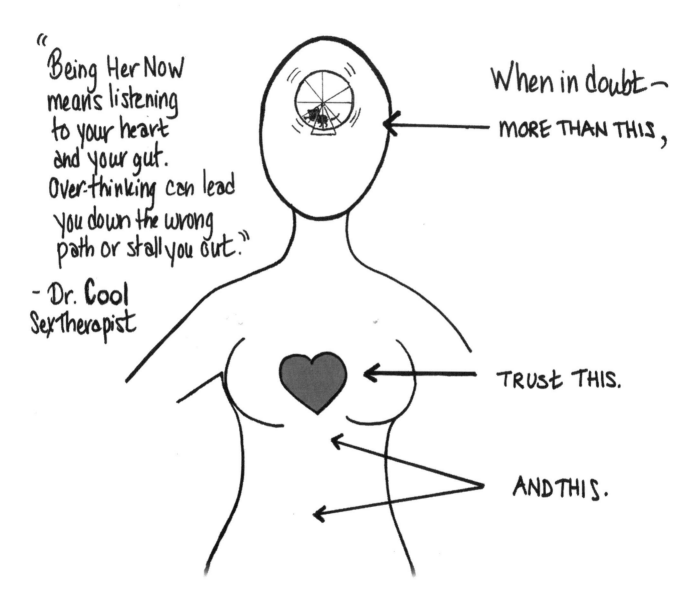

"Being Her Now means listening to your heart and your gut. Over-thinking can lead you down the wrong path or stall you out."

- Dr. Cool Sex Therapist

When in doubt —
MORE THAN THIS,

TRUST THIS.

AND THIS.

"When I hear the words 'Be Her Now,' it immediately brings me to my center, and it reminds me to be who I want to be at that moment. It means that I do not wait for Her to arrive or wait to become Her. I am Her now. It reminds me that I alone choose who I am. It reminds me that I am powerful."

Faye
Tattooed Psychic Heavy Metal Biker Princess

183

"Being Her Now means being who _you_ want to be at any moment."

Sibb - teacher, writer and Michigan Farm girl

" Being Her Now means stepping into the power of my core self, and radiating who I have always hoped to be right now. It means saying I am Her- stunning, wild, free. I am worthy. I am enough. "

– Bunny, Artist Extraordinaire.

Among the women I talked to, there were some common threads:

Be Her Now is both something you are and something you do.

Be Her Now is about trusting, respecting and following your own guidance and your own path.

Be Her Now is about trusting, respecting and LOVING yourself **unconditionally**.

Different situations call out different sides of, and responses in, Her, but that response represents who She is and what She wants in that moment.

But no matter what, Be Her Now means, first and foremost, appreciating and embracing **ALL** of Her – the qualities and tendencies you like in yourself as well as the ones that trip you up or can even make you cringe – without shame or self-consciousness.

No matter who She is, Be Her Now means recognizing that "perfection" is absolutely not the point of the human journey, nor is pleasing, getting along with, or being loved by, everyone else.

And this is a good thing, because for me, Be Her Now sometimes means coming screaming in, hot, fast and low, dropping a payload of truth on someone's ass and then getting the hell out of there before they know what just hit them.

As for you, dear Reader, you **know** who She is. And however far and few between, you've had your own experiences of being Her now, right?

If you're lucky, you have people in your life who truly know you and love you for who you are. They welcome, value, and even insist upon you being HER.

Or maybe you've found yourself in a situation once or twice where pleasing other people and worrying about what they might think if She showed up is decidedly not the point...

A shock of some kind.

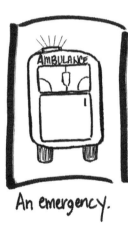

An emergency.

Deep meditation.

...and there **SHE** is.

Present.

Free.

(These are powerful moments, are they not?)

Be Her Now is about making this a way of life.

For most of us, this means we roll in a whole new way.

Our way.

So what does that involve?

What Being Her Now *doesn't* involve is requiring you to buy some "miracle" product off the Internet or do weird stuff like, say, eating nothing but chia seeds and potting soil.

Everything you need to Be Her Now is already within you.

That's the miracle.

Being Her Now is something you learn to do as you go.

It pays not to think of it like a crash diet.

It happens gradually, little by little, moment by moment, being all the Her you can be, day by day, every single day for the rest of your life.

It's not some kind of race or contest, either. It's a course you run in your own way, on your own terms, on your own clock.

There isn't a prize waiting for you at some sort of finish line.

The prize is *in* the doing.

As long as you keep putting one foot in front of the other, staying committed even when you stumble (and you will, again and again) Being Her Now will keep getting easier and easier.

No matter how great an act of imagination this requires of you right now, until you get to the point where being Her is the most natural thing in the world, along the way you practice.

And practice.

You practice and practice and practice and practice and practice and practice and practice and practice and practice and practice and practice and practice and practice and practice and practice and practice and practice and practice and practice and...

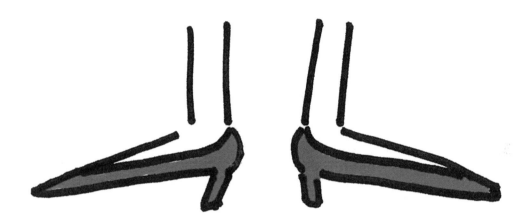

It's like breaking in a new pair of shoes.

You walk around in them until they're so comfortable,
you don't want to wear anything else.

What's that? How are other people going to react to your changes?

I'm glad you asked this question.

Other people – and no surprise here – are the biggest challenge you'll face on your quest to Be Her Now. It's good to have reasonable expectations so that you're prepared going in.

Let's be honest. Living and speaking your truth will piss some people off. You can't be Her and expect everyone to rally around with balloons and confetti, cheering your every bold move.

Parades in your honor?

Not gonna happen.

They will often zero in on the very things you kick your own ass about, which is one of the reasons The Petty can get under our skin, even when we know they're being petty.

So when it comes to The Petty, The Haters and The Critics, here are some things to think about –

We don't live in a vacuum. Exercising the courage to Be Her Now will not only make your own life better. When you are being Her, you encourage the same choice in the women around you. You model this choice for girls. You show them how it's done.

So first – Remember why you're doing this.

Second – being judgey is our biggest weakness as a species, and also our specialty. We criticize each other. We judge. It's just what we do. This means you'll be judged and criticized whether you're trying to please other people or whether you're Being Her Now.

That's one of the **best** reasons for being Her now, the "Why-the-Hell-Not?" reason.

If you're going to be criticized, you might as well be criticized for being Her.

Third – dealing with the Intimidation Factor:

Haters and Critics will often be angry, loud and scary when they talk shit about you. "Angry," "loud" and "scary" does not mean "right." It means "discussion is not even possible at this time," let alone necessary.

Be advised and act accordingly.

And whatever you do, do not turn against yourself in these moments.

Because if you do?

You will invite pain you don't want, need, or deserve into your heart.

This will drain your vital energy.

And you will not be at your best nor offer your best to others.

What about the people who are particularly close by? Family members? Intimate partners? Your kids?

Special discussion.

This is where Being Her Now can get particularly dicey and challenging.

Think of these relationships as a dance.

Let's say you're doing the Fox Trot, just Fox Trotting along with someone close in your life. Then let's say you get inspired to start doing the Texas Two Step...

Possible Consequences:

1.

YAY!!!
I LOVE
THE
TEXAS
2-STEP!!!

Best of all possible
worlds!

2.

Oops!
What's going
on here?
Texas 2 Step?
Oh, okay.
Gimme a
sec here...

Simple confusion
followed by
adjustment.

3.

Oh, HELL no!
We're doing
the foxtrot.
Foxtrot! Foxtrot!
Foxtrot Bitch,
or I will leave
your ass on
the dance floor!

Newton's
3rd Law.

When one person changes, the whole dynamic between people changes. If you switch from Fox Trotting to the Texas Two Step, the other person dancing with you will react, one way or the other.

They might be uncomfortable.

They might not like it.

They might bitch and complain and demand "things go back to the way they were before."

It can take time for people close to you to adjust to your changes. Until they do, you might feel uncomfortable, too.

These are both reasonable expectations.

But you already know this. In fact, it's the very reason we're inclined to shut Her down in the first place, to keep Her inside.

Bad reactions to Her from people we care about are precisely what we fear most. They slam us right up against the walls of our programming.

So it is reasonable to expect that you will consider retreat, the strategy of "Peace at Any Cost."

When it comes to being Her now, these are the moments of truth. These are the times when you must leave your comfort zone and do something different.

Old habits die hard, sure. But they have to *die*. You are going to have to hold them underwater till the bubbles stop coming up.

Remember – being Her now and how other people respond to Her are two different things.

Remember – It's not your job - nor your place - to control how other people respond to Her.

Remember – being Her now means it's no longer the Prime Directive to please other people and make them feel comfortable.

Being Her now means you respect the rights of others to make their own choices.

They're on their own journey, just like you.

Treasure the ones who stick around. Be as compassionate as you can toward those who don't. Love them from a distance if you must.

Easier to say than do, right?

Look, when those moments arise (and they will)
where you feel that urge to cave in and retreat, to start
pleasing people...

WWSD?

(**W**hat **W**ould **S**he **D**o?)

That's right – **What Would She Do?**

When you feel the urge to retreat, that's the question you need to ask yourself.

Nothing, and I mean **nothing**, will get you in touch with Her faster.

Whatever your answer, do that.

"WWSD?" lets you step outside yourself, away from some of the emotional chaos and confusion and fear you feel when you slam up against the walls of programming and old habits.

When you ask yourself WWSD, you look at yourself and the situation through **HER** eyes and you respond like your very own BFF, with compassion, empathy and care.

We aren't hard on our BFFs the way we are hard on ourselves. We can be a complete dumbass about our own lives, but when it comes to our friend, we care foremost about what's right for her, not what will please or upset the people around her. When it comes to our BFF, the saner and healthier choices for her are obvious to us.

When we ask ourselves "WWSD?" the same sort of thing happens.

I wrote "WWSD" on my hand every day for a year using a black Sharpie. I highly recommend this. Try it now!

"WWSD." The creative possibilities are simply endless...

SOME FINAL THOUGHTS...

The most courageous act is still to think for yourself. Aloud.[1]

— Coco Chanel

Some Final Thoughts

The fight against sexist oppression isn't over. Not anywhere. Not by a long shot.

As within, so without.

In the greater project of the liberation of women, equality and freedom for women in the macrocosm goes hand-in-hand with exercising that freedom in our personal lives, on the playing field closest to our hearts.

The Personal is Political.

Decades ago, this rallying cry of the Women's Liberation Movement drew attention to the fact that the problems and frustrations women were facing in their daily lives were a direct reflection of the beliefs, practices and policies of the culture at large.

The political is also personal.

Deeply so.

Sexist policies and practices at large are affected by our priorities, our practices and the choices we make every single day.

Because here's the deal.

Sexism is alive and well and living in our own psyches as much as anywhere else. It keeps us down. It holds us back. It keeps us afraid and distracted and worried over things that do not serve us in any way. It makes us feel smaller than we are.

We cannot afford to relax our vigilance against this tenacious social evil on any front where it exists. That means we have to recognize how the reality of sexism continues to be lived out in the mundane details and choices in our daily lives and in our relationships with the people who share them.

Every time you exercise the courage to Be Her Now, you release yourself more from crippling self-scrutiny and the tyranny of meaningless, wrong-headed and oppressive standards for "acceptable" feminine behavior.

Every time you exercise the courage to Be Her Now, you move forward in realizing the full measure of your own humanity and in being of greater service to others.

As women who are among the most privileged and free women on the planet, it's our responsibility to get over our shit and do this, because the exercise and experience of freedom in our lives directs our attention even more keenly toward encouraging and defending the freedom of all women.

Putting Her on the outside, in charge of our lives, where the world will see Her and hear Her, is an important and significant step in that direction.

Love Yourself.
Be Yourself.
Be Her Now.

The world is waiting.

Notes

Epigraph.

1. "Mohadesa Najumi Quotes," Goodreads, accessed January 12, 2017, https://www.goodreads.com/author/quotes/7754869/Mohadesa_Najumi.

Introduction.

1. Gloria Steinem, *Revolution from Within: A Book of Self-Esteem*, 2nd ed. (Boston: Little, Brown & Company, 1993), 3.

Part One: Our Story.

1. Virginia Woolf, "An Unwritten Novel," in *Monday or Tuesday: Eight Stories* (Mineola: Dover Publications Inc., 1997), 25.

2. Betty Friedan, *The Feminine Mystique*, 4th ed. (New York: W.W. Norton & Company, 1997), 439.

Part Two: Who Is She?

1. "Tina Turner Quotes," Read Print, accessed May 27, 2017, http://www.readprint.com/quotes-2964/ Tina-Turner-quotes.

2. "Oscar Wilde Quotes," BrainyQuote, accessed March 15, 2014, https://www.brainyquote.com/authors/oscar_wilde.

3. Abraham Maslow, "A Theory of Human Motivation," *Psychological Review*, 50 #4 (1943), 370-396.

4. Abraham Maslow, *Motivation and Personality*, 1st ed. (New York: Harper and Brothers, 1954).

5. Viktor Frankel, *Man's Search for Meaning*, 4th ed. (Boston: Beacon Press, 2006), 77, 79-80.

Part Three: Be Her Now.

1. Candy Darling, *Beautiful Darling: The Life and Times of Candy Darling, Andy Warhol Superstar*, directed by James Rasin (2011; New York, NY: Corinth Films Inc., 2011), http://www.netflix.com.

Epilogue: Some Final Thoughts.

1. "Coco Chanel Quotes," Great-Quotes, accessed February 21, 2018, http://www.great-quotes.com/quotes/author/Coco/Chanel/pg/3.

References

BrainyQuote, "Oscar Wilde Quotes." Accessed March 15, 2014, https://www.brainyquote.com/authors/oscar_wilde.

Frankel, Viktor. *Man's Search for Meaning.* 4th ed. Boston: Beacon Press, 2006.

Friedan, Betty. *The Feminine Mystique.* 4th ed. New York: W.W. Norton & Company, 1997.

Great-Quotes. "Coco Chanel Quotes." Accessed February 21, 2017. http://www.great-quotes.com/quotes/author/Coco/Chanel/pg/3.

Maslow, Abraham. "A Theory of Human Motivation," *Psychological Review*, 50 #4 (1943), 370-396.

Maslow, Abraham. *Motivation and Personality.* New York: Harper and Brothers, 1954.

Rasin, James, dir. *Beautiful Darling: The Life and Times of Candy Darling, Andy Warhol Superstar.* 2011; New York, NY: Corinth Films Inc., 2011. http://www.netflix.com.

ReadPrint, "Tina Turner Quotes." Accessed May 27, 2017. http://www.readprint.com/quotes-2964/Tina-Turner-quotes.

Sand, Morris. *That's Ugly.* New York: Pocket Books Inc., 1965.

Steinem, Gloria. *Revolution from Within: A Book of Self-Esteem.* 2nd ed. Boston: Little Brown & Company, 1993.

Woolf, Virginia. "An Unwritten Novel." In *Monday or Tuesday: Eight Stories.* Mineola, NY: Dover Publications, Inc., 1997.

Acknowledgments

I want to thank the following people, who made it possible for me to write this book, who showed up, right on time, with the right words and the exact support I needed at the exact moment I needed it. You are why I know my life rains Pixie Dust.

First, Kim Rich. Peanut, you coaxed an admission from me that "there's this book I've been working on but it might be shit …," insisted I tell you about it and then lost your fucking mind. You are the most generous writer I know. I have never doubted since that day that *Be Her Now* was a worthy project.

The Biscuit, Jim Kendall. You were the one who suggested I draw it. Genius. You were there, laughing with joy and appreciation when the most important and meaningful work I have ever done came into being. "Thank you" doesn't even cut it.

To my family, who didn't hate it. No. In fact you liked it and gave me your unconditional support, my brother, Richard Paulson, especially. I love you to death, man. You are my blood, my home, the one I have known forever. No one else stands where you do in my life or in my heart.

To Mariah Oxford. You were an enthusiastic fan of *Be Her Now* early on, showing me what was possible, pointing me in the right direction, and giving me advice on tools I would need along the way. You asked the right questions. You trusted I could do it. You are one of the most gracious (and sanest) people I know.

To Joan Bantz, Faye Mills, Lynnette Duncan, Kurt Marsch and Mother Aya, who told me to quit fucking around when I was, and then showered me with confetti as I moved forward and got shit done. Girlfriend needs accountability, high expectations, kisses and prizes. I thank you for knowing that.

Huge thanks to all who read various drafts of *Be Her Now* – Sharon Sibbald, Leslie Clemente, Tia Demetro, Eric Mouffe, Marike Van Denend, Maggie Hollingsworth (who has been my reader and cheering squad longer than anyone), Aurora Sidney-Ando (Bunny), Mark Faller, Philip Gordon, Jon Crane, Penelope Goforth, Nora Miller, Michelle Mueller, Becky More, my beloved nephews, Andrew and Mark Paulson, Abby Rethwisch, my niece, Hana Fulghum, my wicked cousins Lee Lee Schlaf, Joanie Mathews and Tom Appelquist, Bob Roach, Anne Gallagher, Laurel Davis Mayo, Margaret Connerly, Lou Johnson, Micki Halloran, Jeri Kopet, Ellen Cole, Kristin Jones (The Glitterboots), Tim Rawson, Tracy Stewart, Mei Mei Evans, Jody Renee Lang, Steven Snyder. And Lyn deMartin! Oh Lyn! Who caught me and my critters when we landed in a heap in Santa Fe, where it finally got serious, and was my perfect muse in the high desert these last important months.

Big thanks to Belinda and Max, who gave me not just support and love but a beautiful place to get the work done.

To Miss Ellen Foreman, my brilliant and eagle-eyed editor. You have saved my ass on occasions too numerous to count. Why the hell aren't you writing books??

OMG to the Wizard, Dickon Kent. Your genius! Your skills! Your artistic vision! Thank you from the bottom of my heart for the enormity of what you did for me on this project and for your kind and loving heart. Thank you to that Goddess, my sister, Molly, for marrying you and bringing you and Bruno into my life. Thank you, Molly, for your strength, your tender heart, for making me laugh really hard, for your support and sound advice and for having my back.

To Anelise Schutz, digital graphic designer/stylist, who was psychic when it came to my vision, as well as being a consummate professional, a genius and a damn machine. How do you do it, grrrl?? I think you may be The Pixie Herself.

Last but not least, to The Baba, Ram Das, author of *Be Here Now*. You were an early inspiration for obvious reasons and in obvious ways. It would be the greatest honor to place Her in your hands. Here's hoping I get to do that.

About the Author

She is a teacher, a storyteller and a liar. She eats too much candy. She will eat your candy and lie about it. She loves lizards, dogs and cats. She is afraid of spiders, horses and clowns. She is a Howler Monkey and is not sorry for it. She lives in Santa Fe, New Mexico. She has not yet been to prison. She can be reached at www.behernow.com.

Made in the USA
San Bernardino, CA
03 February 2019